Advance Praise

'A poem is born of the in-between: a need to build bridges over what separates the mundane from the universal, the inner being from the outer world, the lived from the hoped for, continents and islands, a toy in a child's hand and the aurora borealis, the country where one grew up and the country one is growing into, the deeply personal and the shared reality.

The bridge builders who achieve this are often called *poets*, the walkways they create are called *poems*, and *poetry* is what happens when they are walked by readers, word by word.

Giti Chandra's wonderful collection, *Setting Traps for Light*, inspires thoughts like these. As the first Indian-Icelandic poet in history, what a gift she brings us with her poetry, inviting us to travel across cultures, landscapes, and experiences – for when a poem is created, distances dissolve.'

– Sjón, poet, and author of *Moonstone* and *The Whispering Muse*

'Whether refracting it through personal lyrics or social and political critiques or apprehensions of the natural world, Giti Chandra shines light on what it is to live at pitch of passionate engagement. To read through this capacious collection is to be embraced and illumined by intelligence and insight.'

– Paul Kane, poet, and author of *Work Life* and *A Passing Life*

'If light were a sonnet and the sonnet about the lived experience of grief and joy, then there would be a book of poems, *this* book of poems. Here is an emotional landscape lit up in painterly detail. The shaping craft of this collection comes from sonnets, in rhyme, in pauses, and in the heart-turning wisdom of couplets – even in poems that are not sonnets.'

– Anannya Dasgupta, poet, and founder of Daily Riyaaz

setting traps for light

GITI CHANDRA

hachette INDIA

First published in 2026 by Hachette India
(Registered name: Hachette Book Publishing India Pvt. Ltd)
An Hachette UK company
www.hachetteindia.com

1

Cover design by Anna Thomas
Author photograph by Gunnar Pálsson

Print ISBN 978-93-5731-489-3
eBook ISBN 978-93-5731-431-2

Hachette Book Publishing India Pvt. Ltd
4th & 5th Floors, Corporate Centre,
Plot No. 94, Sector 44, Gurugram 122003, India

Typeset in Change 11.5/15.5 by R. Ajith Kumar, New Delhi

Printed and bound in India
by Manipal Technologies Limited, Manipal

FSC
www.fsc.org
MIX
Paper | Supporting responsible forestry
FSC™ C043100

For my daughters,
Arshia Eyrún Gunnarsdóttir and Ashali Ásrún Gunnarsdóttir

Contents

LOOSING AND BINDING

LOST AND BOUND

IF THE BRAVE WERE LEGION

FORGING COURAGE

Author's Note

Why beauty

Because beauty is a ferocious beast. It comes at you out of nowhere, reminds you that every day is a wilderness and the neglectful path we walk is an illusion of familiarity. In reality, the unexpected and unknown crouches just out of sight and can leap out at you at any moment, demanding attention and immediate contact. Beauty can swallow you whole, pitilessly, in bone-crunching jaws. It has no agenda, it needs no rationale. It is hungry for you and it smells your unthinking desire miles away. And what defences do you have, really, against such a ravenous creature? You could close your eyes to it, but it would still be there, waiting to pounce; or you could find yourself already inside its belly when you open your eyes – it has taken you unawares, stealthily, like a whale. You could anticipate it and bring your armour along, but you are new and beauty is ancient and it tunnels underneath your fortress of indifference and catches your preoccupied mind with practised claws.

So you see, it is never a fair battle. It can take a while to get over the guilt of feeling pleasure in the midst of sadness because the bark of the birch is silver on the outside and crimson on the inside and it delights you outside your door. You can stop being ashamed of being a shallow, frivolous person whose heavy heart lifts effortlessly at the sight of Esja in the early morning when you miss places the most. It doesn't feel like courage to lose your swirling thoughts in the white flurries that circle outside windows, softening harsh contours and cushioning the fall and descent of things. Indeed, if you asked me what courage was, I wouldn't know, but I can see why the late spring ice filigrees into leaf shapes. And if summer reneges on its promises, then the hills produce dreamscape mists in recompense and this, too, is a bravado of a kind.

Why Poetry

Found poems can be read etched into the landscape and shadowed on things. Writing these out, I called them all 'Courage' and I numbered them, so that I could separate the one about rain driven up the windshield against all laws of gravity from the one about rain on the car window making abstract art out of glacial rivers. I thought the naming and numbering would help distinguish the ones about summer suns in northern midnights from the summer suns that foment rebellion in scorching tropical middays; or the one about gold headscarves which turned out to be about grief from the one about how to live in a world that would end tomorrow in which I found myself back on vanished doorsteps in old neighbourhoods. I failed at all this, as one does when trying to name and number and distinguish and separate. And then one day I failed to capture the early summer light that seemed so exotic to me and managed, instead, to paint the smell of monsoon rain falling on home ground, and I wrote a poem about that, but I didn't call it 'Courage'. I laughed at my ineptness and called it 'Light'. That was in the summer.

And in the winter, I stood on bridges and the frozen river suggested I stop being safe and jump in and be fickle, wind, lose my way. I drove by waterfalls and the cliffs reminded me that you need no vision of the sea to plumb its depths. I looked for reflections in ice and the light skimming off it rendered it opaque and freed me from the fear of being self-mattering, self-sung. Stripped bare trees became feathered backbones, weathered in a courage spring has never known. And this, too, I wrote.

I know what you will say. You will say that these are my own thoughts projected on to silent objects and unresisting nature. That the idea of a sympathetic landscape or symbolic materiality is a Romantic conceit, rightfully discarded as sentimental and trite. You will say that it is an ancient and conventional and boring literary device and moreover, that I have told the story, not just of every person in need of courage ever, but of every writer everywhere. So be it. There is a world of poetry – the good, the inept, the sentimental – and crowded and milling about with fears as the world is, glass and metal and wood and skin and boxes and lamps and cloths and kettles and dirt, light finds its way to each of these and demands that we see. And noting how the motes float in the beam is also courage.

the prospect of loss

When falling out of skies

When Falling Out of Skies

An Easter observation

When falling out of skies
It's best to be a mountain.
Your descent to earth a flow
Of rivers in reverse. A settling
Of stone on soil, a closing
Of spaces between. No fountain
Of might or mercy, but sighs
Etched into the rock face.
A rising of Grace.

To Name a Lost Sea

'Kum'. A word meaning dry.
Today I read that the Aral Sea
(So vast a lake that its name was
More than it was meant to be)
Is a desert now. 'Qum',
Meaning sand. How quickly
We have changed water
To land. 'Karakum', a desert,
Held together by the Amu
And the Syr, rivers both, that fed
This now sanded earth. 'Darya',
A word from our childhoods, said

Most often with 'aansu', or 'daya'.
Let irony feed this reservoir of shame.
The Aral Kum is now a name.

Yellowstone

It seems at Yellowstone Park
The Earth's crust is very thin.
If the world were to end, this
Is where it would begin. And
Just yesterday, they found there's
More fire underneath than they
Thought. And it occurs to me that
No battle is as fiercely fought
As between the need for a thicker
Skin and the burn of fires within.

No peace more dearly bought.

Snow/Fall in Delhi

For a non-autumnal city
The fallings off are phenomenal.
Continents weight the red
Leaves that do not fall here.
Glaciers ride the early

Airs that do not bite.
Magisterial Death strides
Through avenues that do not
Blaze here. Sorrow is the only
Secret pact that this city
Of heat and rain makes
With the drifting down of winter.
Only the flowering of grief
On its roundabout trees,
Falls silent, in riotous flakes.

Simple Rhymes for Difficult Times

Peace be in your streets.
Let no neighbour inspect
Your larder for its meats.
Let no man suspect
Your daughter of eyeing
Mates of other castes.
Peace be in your markets
As people shop between fasts.

May those who consider dyeing
Their cloths in other hues
Choose wisely amongst colours
While paying holy dues.
Peace be in your homes

Where reading stops at sundown
When hiding certain tomes
Means riding until run down.

Let no man be left slumped
On his doorstep, stained.
Let huddles of good folk disperse
Their bloodlust undrained.
Let sunsets carry what reds
We need to light our days
And nations wave what flags
They must, and go their separate ways.

Peace be upon this city
That none need earn their pity.

Pretty Summer Song

When the sky is blue and the grass is green
And the ugliness of power lies unseen
It is so much easier to pretend
The meek will triumph in the end.
The rhyme is simpler, and time is kind,
And rhythm and image come readily to mind.
It is hard to imagine that we shall fail
For surely, surely, good sense will prevail.
How clever is nature, so sweet to deceive
And the powerful are more natural than we believe.

The laws they follow, immutable, until
Exceptions erupt, the law to fulfil.
But summer suns are useful to burn,
And marching ants are waiting their turn.
Entire bodies are devoured in moments.
Ignore, at your peril, summer foments.

Limericks for Seasons of 'hurl[ing] the little streets upon the great'

Sometimes in the morning light
The raven follows the eagle's flight
And lesser feathered fowl like me
Slowly savour our morning tea
And note the passing of the night.
When dreams are few and the night is long
And the days unclaimed by the patient throng
It's good to see the eagle fly
Harried by ravens that sound the sky
Crying shame upon the strong.

The Unhappy People

The unhappy people leave their beds
Neat. Covers flat. Corners straight.
It's not like they would falter

In their aim when they throw
Early morning water into their eyes
To bring themselves awake.
If it were you or me, we'd never see
The crumpled sheet
The pillow askew
After all, the shoes we hurry on
Our impatient feet
Are used to having
Something new
To wake up to.

Partitions

Lines are drawn in many ways
Rivers and seas, mountain ranges
Do it. Deserts are harder to use
And oceans often end in bays
Harbouring those refused
Other shelters, other roofs.
Seas are parted to let the exile through
And red marks so many partitions
In lines and rivulets, veins
On the body of the blue
Earth, ruddied with nations
Riddled with stains.
Walking in streets paved with the dead

The folded hands, the unseeing head
The numbers with zeroes marching abreast
It's easy to stop looking for signs;
The names of roads are rollcalls
Unfolding underfoot, in endless lines.

If Wishes Were Horses

For AÁ

At eight, I guess flying horses
Are what little girls desire.
It isn't so much the strength of the beast
As the wings of drifted snow
The mane afire. They are things
Of feather light and sunset glow,
Ponytails bright tied, with ribbons
The colour of russet horse hide,
Little girls are. And mine has spent
The afternoon on YouTube, bent
Over paper, creasing delicate folds;
As if the careful act of origami holds
The rush of wind in her straining face
The crafting of belief, the power of grace.

In Gratitude to April Wayfarers

A month of poems ends
With a day dedicated to labour.
A month that began
With a day dedicated to Fools.
Therein lies, perhaps, a metaphor
Requiring another set of tools.
Yeats's hammer, pummelling thoughts
Into unity; Eliot's chisel, moulding
Images from handfuls of dust.
The spade of James Wright, folding
Epiphanies into the earth's crust.
Old Bill's tarp stretched over our heads
To catch overweaning ambition;
Ghalib and Faiz, Ludhianvi and Mira,
Solder and weld the self and creation.
But of all the names and works of hands
Those of you, all banded here
Are closest to the bone. You stand
Together and walk the way
From All Fools to Labour Day.

End of the Road

If there's an ocean at the end
Of the street, even the puddles
Seem headed that way. The huddled
Buildings, grey and blue, bend
Their angular corners towards the hills
If the end of the street so wills.
I think, as my feet aimlessly wend
Their way down foreign streets,
That there must be a mountain,
An ocean, a future, to meet.

Tiger Tiger

And then they shot the tigers. It defeats
Me how those who earned their stripes
Stripping the Sultan of his jewels and rings
Carried their greed for carrion and ripe
Red rubies to the cages. In the heat
Of the battle, they did not forget to bring
Home his sword with the tiger hilt;
Kept his tiger throne. The empire built
On death and plunder, cannot cheat
Me of the astounded wonder, at this thing
– I cannot name it, it baffles me –

That moved an army that killed a country
For its jewels, just like the unnamed soldier
Who killed Tipu for his, crowned its glory
By killing the Sultan's six tigers. Bolder
Poets than I have battled with history
Finding rhyme, if not reason. Did they see
What Blake did, burning bright
In those striped lords of war? What
Did they go and kill them for?

(Tipu Sultan was killed in battle by an anonymous soldier for his precious ornaments. After the generals found his body, they took over his fort, and killed his six tigers.)

Courage VI

Things have a way of freezing
Differently. Mountains expose
Their bones, ribs of eruptions past
One over the other, ceasing
Only to fall in line with those
Fault lines spring hides. Fast
And furious run your rivers
Racing ahead of those wintry blasts
Terrified of stiffening into slivers
That once were ripples, tearing
The smoothness of surface ice. Wearing

The grass that cold crisps into blades
The differently freezing earth brings
No herald of bubbling springs. The thaw,
If it comes, will escape on your breath
A defiance of death, the chill air
Your heart warms. Courage is the air
Your frozen blood sings.

loosing and binding

Every loved thing unfamiliar,
every borne grief new

Courage V

With thanks to Anjan Ray for the astonishing image in which
I found this poem

If the road ahead is
Mottled, splotched in
Sun and shade; if
The helm you wear was
Once a net of steel
That held out even as
You held on; if
The green that greets
You slides back into grey,
Courage can be the dust
In the slanting ray.
But sometimes the peace
Of the branchéd tree
Shields your progress
Away from fright.
Promising shelter yet
Ceding ground in
An onslaught of
Unilluminating bright.
Sometimes courage
Is the flight of the bird
Startled out of its darkness
Into the indifferent light.

New

On New Year's day last year
I woke up in a new home. Mine,
But not yet; loved but
Not heart-set; mine,
But a strange bed, a distant view
Of hills bathed in blue
Deep-winter light, a promise
Since redeemed. Mine,
But never before
Known. How we've grown
Accustomed to newness.
Familiar with not knowing how
With what words, what ink
What salutations
To greet this stranger who eats
At our table, quaffs our drink.
Not knowing if naming
Or not naming
Will drive him hence. Not wanting
To lose that which
Is always here. So dear
That no known name
Will ever change
Its forever.
This morning I woke up
In a familiar bed made new. You

Would think that this place
This house where
My children grew
Would need no naming
And part of that is true.
Yet this stranger, craning
Its neck over my shoulder
Erasing each word I write,
Who, running beside me knew
The ache of muscles in my stride
From ship to ship, port to port
Racing from one home to another
Desperate to outpace him
This stranger has forever
Made every loved thing unfamiliar
Every borne grief new.
How may I unname him
Let me count the ways.
Not death nor loss nor absence
Or love, not sorrow nor grief
No song no poem no light above
Nor ground beneath
Nothing special or specific
Neither unique nor new
Not such that is bequeathed
To only me or even a few
Named every moment, called
Every name, beseeched

By every heart it ever threw
Always everywhere and forever
All of this is true.
Yet it has made every loved thing
Unfamiliar, every borne grief
New.

Sing Me No Songs of Consolation

Slivers of sky string
Their silver blue through
Green and rock, stones
Strewn in their path like
Little clouds, as if to sing
To me their broken tones
Of consolation. But
Who will bravely bring
The riverbed forth. The gravel
And sand of dry grief. Who
Will raise pebbles smooth as bone
Unwritten, unscratched. What thief?
Who dare to build that dyke
That will dam the waters and read
On them their smooth, unwritten,
Consolation.
If there is such a one,
To that sturdy soul I say,

Show me the pebble, worn
As my heart, one among millions
And wring from that single stone
The river that runs from me, one
Among millions. Build me that
Single dam that will make
Of that river a lake
One, among millions,
Where I may stop, and leaning,
See no face but my own, broken
As only mine is, as a river
Washes through me, a mirror
For no grief but my own.
Until then, sing me no songs
Of consolation, no hallelujahs
Of pain sung before. I take
No comfort in the lake
Of another's tears.
Raise me that stone, dam me that lake,
Name the face that weeps into those waters.
There are fathers enough, I know,
And no dearth of daughters,
Yet I take no solace from the songs
Of bereavement that they make.
Like a primordial flood the
Massed choirs sing of loss and losing
And drown each daughter's voice
Added without her choosing.

And I, who have no other choice,
Silent as I hold this dam against
The breaking of that deluge, I,
Who reach into the deep only
To throw back stones I cannot
Keep; I, who float,
Face up, like the dead, and reach
For clouds that lie like stones
That lie, that sing, that preach
But have nothing to teach
Me, nothing to place
In my palms, facing upward.
I slip silently under boats that
Skim the waters, their keels
Humming, and think – you,
Who are on the boats, you
Whose shirts do not fill
With waters that run through
You; you, whose fingers strain
The river as you glide through pain
You liars, deceivers, dealers in
Consolation. I want
No part of you. I hear
Your songs but they are not
Mine. Your tears
Fall on my face but they
Are not mine. I cannot
Fashion a lyre from my breath

Unlcss it bespeak
This death.

To Fall Now

For MS

To fall now would be something.
To plummet into the sky like an eagle
In the glories of the hunt; it's wing
A crescent under the sun. To fall
Now would be a marvel, like death
Screaming out of the blue, awaiting
The tiny shards of life flying apart.
To fall now would be a homecoming
An April shower on trees both alien
And alike: where fear is the falling
And love is the spike.

91 Days

91 days, and still
My dreams are full of leaving.
Just a few nights ago I dreamt
Again, of that last box
That needed to be packed
After all the rest were done

Hundreds and hundreds of boxes
All reduced to this one.
And yesterday it was a suitcase
The last, on the final day;
And in that dream I found
Patent leather shoes, deep maroon,
From maybe twenty-five years ago,
As good as new. So I put them
In too. And strange letters of farewell
From earlier goings away even when
I had come back, to stay.
Night after night I sort through my things
Frantic not to leave anything important
Behind. And through the day
I ransack my dreams, searching
For that desperate something
That escaped all those boxes
Sleepless, to find
What it is that
I've left behind.

No Place Like Home

I walked right into it.
The immense waiting sadness
The nipping-at-the-heels panic
The monster on my back
That I carried through the manic
Chaos of letting go. The madness

Of thinking I could leave.
Walk away.
Thinking I would retrieve
A home I'd packed away
Retracing a leaving only
To find no trace left behind
But of sadness indiscriminate.
And so I walked right into it.
Not knowing that once you've gone
There's no place like home.

The Impossible Stubbornness of Walls

Holding out as time and space and grief
Ravage the holding in. The brazen
Promiscuity of objects that move
To new homes, and glow with the accumulation
Of new-gathered riches. The unthwarted rigour
With which the shape of things cling
To the walls which held them up, the naked nails
Rejoicing in their unreplaced importance.
The returnee is eyed askance: cupboards retaining
The unwanted residue of indecision
Refuse to acknowledge the suitcase
And carry-on items that accompany moving.
Necessity is not the driving force of need.
Items left, undiscardable, regard the rest
As mere luggage. Unstable, movable.
Lightweight air freight.

No, home is never where the heart is. Ask the walls.
The brick and mortar that stand as you walk
Ride and fly where the heart takes you. Cement
Understands immutability. The resistance of immovability.
Make new homes, go. But if you really want to be gone
Use your bare hands to tear those walls down.

Titanic Truths

Before it sank it broke in half.
That's what gets me every time.
Not the coldness of the winter waters
That are a numbing kindness.
Not the unthinking slaughter
Of workers who never got on boats.
Not the ships that never heard
The calls of distress, but the blindness
That never sees that truths come to us broken.
Before they lie silent on ocean floors
Before they lie, truths are always two-fold.
The one part which we let fall, frozen,
And the one part which we hold.

Amaltās

Masks of summers past

The pleasure of daffodils
Worth the words of that couch-lier

Danced springbright until
The light one early evening caught
The shine and glow and fire
Of amaltās. An empty vase
A mirror, a mask – it's not
As if reflections on summers past
Cannot be painted and worn. It's just
That sometimes the pleasure of
The amaltās
Cannot be borne.
The green and gold bronze
The all seeing eye; rivulets
Of yellow run down the ivory cheek.
Of all the things left behind, I
Carried a face to face the lost things
I would seek. It's not
As if reflections of Indian summers
Can't be worn. It's just that sometimes
The memory of amaltās
Can't be borne.

Love Poem

Love is a new city
Walked through street by street
Love is holding hands
Love is aching feet
A new city is uncertain routes

Unhealthy foods, unempty
Seats. A new city is seeing
New things well after you're
Totally trashed and beat.
Love is knowing home is in
Cities old and new when
The journey home is always
Far, and nineteen years too few.

Courage IV

I want to be the rain
That is driven up shields of glass
Against all laws of nature and grief
I want to know that as
I fall from skies shedding legions
Of such as me, over loaded over crowded
Bent on hurtling earthwards, that I
Will rise again, pushed onwards
On wings of air, knowing when
And where, the edge of glass meets
The skies. Not this me
Strapped and seated
Watching the road fly past through
Streaks of water. Strapped
And seated, not
Undefeated.

Warriors II

Sticks and stones, they said,
Will break our bones, and tied
Me to their armoured
Jeep. And I weep
For them, blinded
Without pellets.

Courage II

Or: What the Lady M can teach us on Shakespeare's birthday

'But screw your courage
To the sticking place,' she said,
And I think of my fear as
Something you can embed –
A small, innocuous wooden peg.
Of my grief as a
Finely tuned thing, a string
Instrument, where each
Memory is stretched
Clear and fixed
At its appointed pitch
Across a body delicately
Calibrated, the mind a sturdy
Soundpost, designated
Survivor, carved with incisions

That each anxiety may breathe
And all, in resonated precision
Hum in its wake.
And I take
My fate in my hands
Like a bow on the wing,
And courage is the song
That the strung heart sings.

Cry Me a River

You see that streak in the middle?
That looks like a river? It was actually
A little sliver of rain, just a drop, really,
The only one left after the wind
Had dried the rain that fell constantly
That day. I wanted a picture
Of the mountains streaked with ice
Vivid under the flat grey of the skies
And I didn't see that single streak
Slipping down the glass windscreen
Carving a seeming crevasse on the peak.
You won't notice, unless you're very near,
The mountain, moved by a tear.

Courage I

A daily riyaaz

Dedicated to those
Who save us from our
Lives of prose.
We are those warriors who
Forge weapons from sorrow
From the things that haunt us
From our consolations. From each
Thought too tiny to share, from
Those fleeting visions too
Overwhelming to bear. Our wars
Are those that keep beauty awake
That inch of ourselves that remains
Defiant at the end of the day
And finds that one thing that
Is worth our while to say. So you,
My fellow berserkers, give me
Madness for my armour, my
Bearskin of words, and your open
Hearts that are a battle cry. Our
Voices sing each other's songs
For all our days, never long
Enough to douse that thirst
Till one month ends with
Another month's first.

lost and bound

How to live in a world that will end tomorrow

Love in the Time of Climate Change

It was a drive by shooting. The river
Become rain, and a small
Window of opportunity. White water
Rapidly swirled, a looking glass
Glossed in green. So swift, this bridge.
Ah love, let us be true
To one another, as the good poet said.
Let us make such slow melting love
That the glacier itself should blush
At its haste, it's blue demise a rush
Of warmth and waste. Let us savour
The centuries old taste of tossing our gods
Into waters already falling, no longer
Chaste. Our love shall be a raft, fuelled
By no heat, in a world bent on burning.
Deserts and dry continents are no grounds
For deserting. We shall find our feet
To a love of no returning.

Courage VII

If the road you're on should
Curve along the waters, and
The only light is far out on
The sea, I hope the answering

Greys of the skies sing with
The voices of distant eyes
And places where you long
To be. And if the flight of
Feet should bring you oceans
Unshored, leave you without
Bridges, unmoored, I wish you
Clouds both light and dark,
Where courage is the mist you
Hold as you fasten your fear
To your barque.

How to Live in a World That Will End Tomorrow

You go to the sidewalk and you
Call out a name any name that
Comes first to your mouth you
Don't look north you don't
Look south it's all the same at
The beginning of the end everyone's
Your friend the guy frying eggs
On a thela by the street omelettes
People buy in a hurry to eat the
Kid kicking cans in a fenced off
Lawn the women eyeing the
Flip flops that you had on because
You knew there wasn't going to

Be a dawn that this heartbreaking
Sunset was just another con why
Would the threadbare family care you're
Just passing through they live
There on the edge of paths that
Pass them by blowing out clouds that
Blot out the sky you should think twice
If you're going to do this think of all
The great stuff you're going to
Miss the house you won't step into the
Fields you'll never see the trick of
The light that makes you think you're
Prettier than you used to be but the
Time has come you've had your
Walk no leisure left to stop take stock the
World will end tomorrow and you
Should call out a name so that the
Monsters in the morning will know
Whom to claim.

Brimketill, Reykjanes

Why do they let it go, the sea,
Back to its roil and tumble
The clefts, the nooks, the craggy
Holes can't seem to hold on to
The rushing blue and white the

Blackness of the rocks darker
As they let it slip through
Their fingers, tears down the faces
Of cliffs. Why do they not keep
The frantic waters sheltered in
Steep hollows, shallows with no
Traces of the deep, silent
Holding its grief in sleep. Why would
The ocean crash into stony
Arms if its heart was not bent
On seeking its keep.

Gullfoss in December

Frozen falls like continents dropping
Off the edge. Cliffs unable to hold
The catastrophe at bay, raise rock fingers
To clutch the long end of Africa. Fire
And ice, didn't they say, would conspire,
To tear it apart – the work of eons, so
Painfully pieced together. Nothing now
To tether the ancient pieces to each other.
Let them go, watch as they crumble.
Maybe another world, another god
Will catch them as they tumble into
The crevices of time; wonder at the species
What fury, what arrogance, what crime

Dismantled the earth's crust. Unclasped
The pin that held it in trust.

Unnameable I

Not that many years ago, I wrote
A poem for my daughter who was eight
How she spent hours making paper
Horses. The delicate art of
Origami concentrating her young frame
The wind in their manes a kind of grace.
Today another eight year old face
Asks me how little feet flying
Over hills and grass with a herd
Of horses in her care, are now lying
In a grave seven kilometres away
From a resting place denied her
When the only grace granted her
Was dying.

Unnameable II

I remember when my girls were small,
I trained myself never to say their hands
Were soft as flowers. Or that their faces
And smiles and dancing figures brought

To mind roses or lilies or stalks of tall
Rajnigandhas. Not even the thought
Was allowed to enter my heart. A heart
In whose depths lay a memory so wild
'She was like a flower, my little child'
A mother whispering of her girl, 2002.
I will never – am never allowed to – forget you.

Un(en)titled

These are the races of people:
Those who hope to love
And those who need to hate.

These are the tribes of people:
Those who defend the powerful
And those who defend the weak.

These are the castes of people:
Those who are attacked in libraries
And those who burn books.

These are the religions of people:
Those who kill for their gods
And those who die for their beliefs.

These are the broken bones and blinded eyes of people, the bloodied shirts
And shattered cries of
People, the invaded homes and bolted gates of
People, the denied countries, refuge, and states of people,
The detained people and blood and grime
Stained people, the pressed into service by power
People, the made to kneel and cower people, our
People:

Those that are glorified and killed
And those that are vilified and killed.

On the Burning of Cathedrals

Grand cathedrals burn down. It is in
The nature of things. Greatness seems
To mark beauty, at the edges, to
Singe. As if destruction sculpted the body of
The old, as if the stealing were in the
Glory of the gold. Palmyra was flattened
They say, even statues brought down
And levelled with the grey of sand. Entire
Cities stand witness to time in their falling.
In the Museo Nacional they found – amid the
200 million treasures lost – a human skull. The
Oldest human, Luzia, like a book recovered from

That blaze of human history, Alexandria,
Survived like a photograph from a vacation album,
Taken, oh, a few years ago – we remember the exact
Year and day – of us, standing, see? right there,
You can see it looming behind the kids, the
Unfallen spire, I can't believe we'll never
See it again, such a place! – Such is the nature
Of human desire, fueled into passion by
Such a lie. How seductive it is, to see things
Die. To know that the histories of Iraq were
Scattered to bidders in various lands. To feel
The contours of cathedrals that live now, only
In our hands.

'You are the way and the wayfarers'

has
Stayed in my heart for as long as I
Can remember. The traveler who stumbles
In warning to those behind, and in reproach
Of those gone ahead. Teach your children well,
They say, or the silent reproach of those behind
Might not even survive the thin ice or live to
Tell. You can do it [your] way, take
The road less travelled, call it another
Lonely day, but for the sake
Of the beauty of the way, and the goodness of

The wayfarers, I wonder if the thronged
Thoroughfare, with its stumbling stones waiting
To be removed, doesn't have a strong
Claim on those of us who lay such store by
The words of those who went before.

Watch Tower 14

If you died building the wall, they say,
You were buried within it. Upright, maybe,
So you could still see the enemy coming
And stand your ground. Or, if you lay,
Your hands folded, perhaps, you could count
The soles of hurrying feet. Windows and
Arches open the sky in shapes of fear that
Slide along the walls of Watch Tower 14.
Hills of blue and square skies threaten to fall
On the reclining or upright dead, like enemy
Feet, with truncheons and knives. A wall
Is such a fragile veil between living
Deaths and dying lives.

The Magnolia Tree

I watched him set up his tripod
So careful, so minute, so intent

And certainly the tree deserved
Every lens positioned, head bent
For long moments – the perfect focus
Of eye and hand, of pure blent
White bloom and winter light.
How tangible the clasp of beauty
And love. I stood so long watching
That I never saw the group of women
Posing. Laughing, jostling, they called
To him to take the picture, to hurry
As they stood under the lovely tree.

Hraundrangi

For Marshu

There's a lake there, just at the
Foot of the crags. Every time I
Pass this way I think I'mma make
It there. I know what you're
Thinking. I need to lose fifty pounds
Get new knees, put in some serious
Cardio at the gym. I know it sounds
At best, grim. And I hear you. But
That water is deep and still, and
It sees that tortured hill and it
Takes it to its heart and sends
It back to its surface, beautiful

And blue. So I'm going to wend
My way there, weary or not. There's
A path, I've seen it, it doesn't seem
Too tough. I've fought my way
Through tougher. There's not a thing
That lake can't compensate me
For whatever I might suffer.

A Whitsun Song for the Road

For Girish Karnad

Tell me why the road needs a song;
It isn't a winding river shining
In the sun. Tell me why it brings
Hidden meanings to the pen, unbidden
Yearnings that flock to the fore and when
The road turns, the wanderer in you
Learns how much you long for beauty
Without the thorns. Tell me why,
Now that Karnad is dead, the road
Might meander away from where
He led. Tell me stories mile-stoned
By the rocks you hurl into
The way ahead. Now that Gibran
Is gone from our memories and our
Libraries change their histories, tell me
Who will collect, catalogue, call

Our songs of those blocks where we
Stumble and fall. Tell me why we sing
Our heartbreak when the roads we take
Are the driven-paved paths we make.

For All the Signs

that
Follow the streets – signalling
Turns and dangerous bends -
The road forever skirts the
Feet of hills lightening
Slowly into the sky. First
The mountain that wends its
Stony way into my path, and
Shadowy, effacing their earthy
Bodies, another two – smudges
On the sky.
Would three days suffice me
Three ways guide and advise
Me; would three mountains
Inscribe me, their stones and
My feet a story to rewrite me.
So many deaths and I
Have learnt no truths. No lies
Can save and revise me.
Come on, resurrection. Roll back

Your stone. Raise your reborn
Head and surprise me.

Objects in the Mirror

You steady them as one
Pudgy foot struggles to not
Plop itself onto the other in
The giant effort of will towards
Forward propulsion. And later,
Moving from three wheels to
Two, you hang on to seat and
Handle, the careening and
Shrieking and scraped knees
Testimony to the onward progress
Of infant navigation. You might
Guide a horse through its paces,
Trim a sail, fix a roller or blade
On a skate, all in service of
An ongoing momentum, but then
They're at the wheel and you
Need to teach them to reverse.
Rear view and side mirrors suddenly
Warn that things behind you
Are closer than they seem. Use
Them anyway, you say, don't turn
Your head don't look back you're

On four wheels now not three or
Two and you know there's no
Cutting them any slack no free
Bridges to burn its life or death
Now kid, and there's only one
Or the other ahead so learn
To use your mirrors to look
Behind you to remember
Everything you've been taught
About moving on. You'll never
Know where you arrive if
You don't hold on to
Your drive.

Anniversaries

Keeping score

The girls are making us an anniversary dinner. Remember
When we mashed bananas and pears for their
Toothless selves to eat? Fed them from purple
Hippo and green turtle plates with frog-bibs?
The years we careened about the countryside, hectic
And frazzled, impossible commutes, every day
A composition of carefully controlled chaos
Culminating in the culinary calm of dinner. And each
Year, aunts, uncles, cousins, siblings, siblings-in-law,

Nieces, nephews, parents, friends, and yes, kids,
congregating
To eat, laugh, cut cakes, sit around, conferring, debating,
Dinner long past, till everyone left, lingering at the gate
The cars gently departing, leaving the lane to its late-night
State. Remember the Blue Frog – just us, a dinner date?
How many dinners make a score of years, anyway? Some
May say 365 into twenty's plenty. Me, I smell the cooking,
hear
The giggling, wait for you to be done with the gymming,
take
Another look at the mehndi picture, and my dear, like
A good appetizer, this is just the beginning.

if the brave were legion

Now that our masks have revealed us

Courage I

Some days I am the frozen lake
Peaceful amidst strong hills
Some days I am the petulant sun
Determined to go where I will.
The other day, I was the laden cloud
Shattered by epiphany
My brooding greys split black and white
My single sharded to many.
Today I am the jagged edges
Of shorelines uncertain and sharp
Pulling away from towering pledges
Shadowed from the bright-lit heart.
I wonder if the lake I was
Runs, still, beneath the crust
If courage is not the water's edge
Meeting what shores it must.

Blood on the Tracks

Think how deep a sleep must be
To not hear a train coming. How weary
Must be the bones to not feel the tremor
In the steel rails. How mighty must be
The weight of the kilometres walked
In daylight, how heavy the limbs curled

Into themselves; how filled with longings
The small pillow of worldly belongings
That cushion the head paused in flight
From the certain knowledge of death
In the restful reaches of the night. Think
Of the poet who said it shall all be
Remembered. The washed away art
The slippers of women removed, the living
Soul of us, like these bodies, dismembered. Think
How we daily forfeit the right to our grief
Our surprise our shame our shock
Our disbelief. Not one of them looks back
No slogans no signs no songs the streets
Are theirs. The empty streets and the blood
On the tracks.

Nessun Dorma

For Nazia, who said she would continue protesting

When you lay your head on
Your pillow tonight, weary
From the labours of the day;
When you kiss your child on
Her head tonight, and quietly slip
Away; when you call your mother
Because she sounded a little low
When you spoke with her

Yesterday; remind her to rest
Her back, see her doc, take
Her meds, take it slow; when
You settle in to work a bit, preparing
For a full day ahead;
Spare a thought for the woman, out
On the street, keeping vigil over
Your humanity, sitting in peace, dry
Eyed, mourning her dead.

May Day Mayday

How may we labour
To save ourselves?
Shall we gather about us
Bulwarks of uncertainty
To guard us from future
Arrogance? Shall we collect
Images of unaccommodated mankind
That we may be protected
From fears of ennui, enclosed
In our own four walls. Will
The memory of mountains
Not seen in decades ensure
Our survival as a species?
For myself, I call forth
The blazing amaltās that

Flame the streets of my city
That their fire consume the
Distance between us, and
Refine my relief to pity.

Now That Our Masks Have Revealed Us

How curious, this motley masquerade
To sashay forth in some carnival's
Parade as if the gold and dazzle and points
Of lace could present to the crowds some
Other soul, an alien head, a faerie face.
What deception is left to practise now
When we hide ourselves from neighbours
And friends. Will we know each other, when
This ends, or shall we hear each stranger ask
Who are you now, without your mask?

'And not by eastern windows only'

I read it first when I was twelve,
A poem my father remembered from
His early days in school. I'm not sure
What he was thinking but we spoke of it
Often over the years. Battles waged and lost
Wars that ended in tears, hope was always

The prize. Because the quality of light
Perhaps, is also twice blest, touching
Those who are beaten and those who wield
The batons of power with the same
Vision of unrest. Every woman sitting
Through the night, every student braving
Authority's might, every migrant
Shouting against the roar, every
Citizen courting arrest – they know
Why they fight, they know what this
Is for, they know why they persist. Hope
Is the only reward of all those who resist.

Ode to the Ordinary

(Because Shelley)

Hail to thee, O Ordinary Thing! Beloved
Thou never wert! If of thee I must sing
To the Romantics I must revert. Because
Seriously, who even notices a handshake,
Buying bread, passing people in the hall
Whose eye you avoid if you look at them at
All? High fives, fist bumps, chatting with
An office-mate, having to trudge to lunch
Another building, same office bunch-huddle
Close in the elevator discussing what you
Ate. Yes, it is sublime, in its

Way, the unwashed beauty of the
Ordinary day, the unnoticed, unapplauded
Transience of the repetitively mundane
The ubiquitously profane.
Say it now in romantic rhyme
The Ordinary is the Skylark of our time.

Courage VIII

Like a false dawn, the late winter snow
Beckons and seduces, shaping itself into
Leaves, coyly clinging to dry branches too
Embarrassed to admit to their saplessness.
See how the melting snow, like a lost love,
Shines the timid light, the brittle lace of
It chasing the gaps into glimmers of
Haplessness. Just for a moment, as you
Pass it by, it holds its dying in mid-air,
A newly shaped bud, unleafed and bare.
Courage is not the coming of Spring;
It is the promise of grace late winter
Will bring.

'Please state the nature of the medical emergency'

I am afraid I will die.
Really? Here in your lovely

Voluntary exile, hibernating with
Your plants and your music and your
Elegant lounging style?
I am afraid to die. Aren't
We all this is hardly
An emergency. I am afraid to live.
When everyone has died. Seriously
Too many bad movies is hardly cause
To summon the emergency medical
Hologram please state the
I am afraid to live as if everyone is dead.
There was that so hard? Why not just
Say so? Instead we have all this
Bleating about dolphins returning and
The new blue of the skies – true, some
Of it, but mostly photoshop and lies
I'm also afraid – oh there's more? Where
Does it hurt I'm sure there's a cure – that
I'm relieved to not be able you see there
Is news of thousands walking beaten
Stuffed into boxes and starving and I
Unable my hands are tied I'm self
Isolated you see couldn't help if I
Tried but my fear is not a symptom it's
Really my relief I'm afraid to have to
Add conviction to belief. There. Lie down.
What you're experiencing is grief. For all
That has died around you and all

You will kill there's not much
I can do for you but I will
Say this: as much as you may say that
You want this to end, get back to your
Work, meet a real friend – grief will always
Urge you to pretend that
You got this you can do this everything's
On the mend. This shall pass too.
So lie down. Things will
Die down. As death tends to do.

Twelve

For Jamalo Madkam, twelve, who died walking the four hundred km march home

– not a number you associate with
The age of the dead. Four hundred – not a
Measure of kilometres you think of as lying
Ahead. Hundreds of thousands – an amount
That exceeds the space in my mind, so many
Hearts beating that when one of them burst, even
Its silence seems impossible to find. How do we
Claim to think of ourselves as one, a number
So invisible that we may never know its kind.
How will we account for fares unrefunded,
Trains unboarded, homes unreached, the lives
Discounted, the peace unbreathed, the pity

Unspoken. One, a number divisible only by itself
On every step of every long march home
Lies broken.

The Measure of Debt

How sweetly sleep the tree-lined streets
That guide the city's weary. Unbearably
Light their burden tonight, the thin-soled
Steps of the unchosen in flight. How sweetly
Scented and cleanly airy the lone highways
Under the cool moon's light, their painted lines
Barely marking the grime of thousands of
Footprints crossing the white. How sweetly
Flows the river blue through the city as it used
To do, rippling our endless thirst for beauty
That is our civilizational right. Spilt milk shared
By animals and men who bend their mouths
To the dark asphalt, sunrise placing of hunger's
Hope mark the tar six feet apart. It used to be
That the beauty of death was that all it asked
Was six feet of ground. It used to be we kept
In sight the measure of debt owed to Beauty's
Might.

On Reading That the Water of the Ganga is Clean Enough to Drink Again

They say the water of the holy river
Is clean enough now for people to drink. They
Would have us believe that cleansing it
Is actually much more important than
We think. That the blood in my veins runs
Thicker, that the life it gives burns quicker,
That the trail we leave is slicker than a burst
Oil tanker, more life-giving than the bloodless
Bodies that no longer feed the divine demands
Of the river. Maybe it is. Maybe tributaries
And streams collect our mortal remains, our
Little dirty dreams, immersed in our fossil-fueled
Caves, no unclogged channel that drains our
Over-flowing hearts. That holy river has its own
Source, it doesn't need our bodies but it asks
Them of us that it may run its course. Death and the
River are reluctantly parted, the more we die, the
Less we understand how all this started. And we,
Who knows where hope springs who knows
What tomorrow brings. All we can see is this
Water and this blood run together unconsecrated
In this unprecedented flood.

For All Those Sending Food to the Unhoused on the Long Road Home

You can tell you're home because they feed you.
Bowls and platters filled in love fried and sautéed and
Curried by hand each spice and grain and leaf
Chosen with care because you're home and they need you
To know how good it is to have you in the circle
Of their arms, out of harm's way. You could say
That this recent splurge of breads and cakes
Exotic recipes, tender meats, and aromatic
Bakes is a circling of arms about ourselves,
A reaching up into neglected cupboards to
Shake a little love from tins on our shelves. Such
A strange thing, food. Hastily wrapped
Meals, made by strangers for nameless strangers
Trapped between the leaving and the returning
So many unhoused each one unknown. Such a
Strange thing, food, delivered in packets,
Hundreds at a time, carrying the promise of home.

When Old Men Die

We try not to think of our fathers. How they,
At this age or in this shirt or with that
Grey stubble on their now less frequently shaved chin,
Speckling a bonier jaw, a slacker jowl, a scrawnier neck,

Would look. We try not to meet that old man's
Eye. How the sockets are drawn in, how
It seems shinier somehow, intent on your face
So as to read your thoughts perhaps anticipate
Your rejection your already-forgiven guilt
Your patience already wearing thin. We try
Not to listen to the intensity of their speech
How it repeats its urgent injunctions, its requests, its
Generous bequests. When old men die
We try not think of our fathers
As a man who dodders where he stands. A man
Who built a nation with his hands.

Verdict

You can pack it in cylinders. Go to
ICUs when disease grips your throat.
When straining will not sift it
Into your lungs. It bewilders
The mind to have to compete,
So complete is the irony that we
Fight for air. Who will shift it
This knee on our neck, face down,
Grit on cheek, no breath to speak,
No bed to sleep on, etherised
In our castles, safe in locked

Towns. Should we be surprised
Sing hallelujahs, when murder
Most foul is recognized and
Gavels bang down a verdict
Of guilt in these life-giving, blood-
Spilling grief-bringing cities
That we have built.

Six Degrees of Three Million

Three million. That's the count – some say a tenth
Of the total dead. Let's play a little game: six
Degrees separate us from any person on earth,
Yes? We all know this one, or at least have heard
Of someone who does – or someone who knows
Someone who knows etcetera. It's a tiny dent
In our sense of isolation or insulation or whatever
It is that keeps us safe inside our skins. So
Let's play. Let's say that if those three million knew
Another three million who knew another six times
Over - my math may not be sound but stay
With me – let's say that you see where I'm going
With this. We are all separated only by six degrees
From any one of those three million. Where
In this net of small crimes will any of us hide
Once we see that one-sixth of each of us has died.

Earth Day Song for the First Day of Summer

The Loðvíðir proclaims – summer is come.
Not yet, say the hills, not yet. The whiteness
Of snows is not ready to pass into your
Branches. My buds are bright already,
Laughs the leaf-bare tree. It is in the
Rightness of things that you should
Let this be. Ah, but they are fur-wrapped,
Grunt the peaks, snug in their mists. Seas
Draw near, grey in their yearning, but
The mountains rein them in, enfold
The reflected clouds in far-away embrace.
Summer is here – the grass loosens its
Hold on it's dreams of green. Not yet, huffs
The breeze that heightens into wind. The
Chill sighs bleak, a memory returning.
Will you remember me when I was
Cold and clear and blue, a winter
Lesson a winter peace a winter worn
That has paid its dues. Let summer
Pink and grasses green but let you
Not think that the winter has passed
You by, unseen.

What Need of Poets

'Come and see the blood in the streets'

What need of poets when pyres are lit
On sidewalks – shall I say 'let us go then,
You and I, when the evening is spread out
Against the sky' and patients no longer
Etherized are strewn in our way? What need
Of imagery for a people starved
Of oxygen? Will metaphor bridge the
Chasm between the living and those
Unable to breathe? Should I not, instead,
Stake out my ground, and as a signpost might,
Point and direct the onlooker to parks
Abloom with pyre-beds, and flames that feed
Oxygen-giving trees with their dead? When
The iron hearts of crematoriums surrender
The poet needs must accept defeat. No mere
Broken heart melting with pity that still
Beats in my wordless body can compete.

For the Trees of Central Vista, New Delhi

Vista
: a pleasing view
: a mental vision of a succession of remembered or
anticipated events.

The dignity of lamps lights them still
Even when felled. The freshly dug pits
Receive them with the compassion of
A mass grave for unaccommodated
Humankind. Their roots do not flail
Naked, expelled from earthy homes.
Their heads do not bow, bending and
Leafy, green amidst sandstone
Domes. No cry no shout no wail
Of iron links sundered from brass
Headed rail no sound of an ending.
So silent, this raising of dust in the
Awkward extraction of the mighty
Stout-as-stone heart of a nation.
Where grief, quiet as smoke,
Stands sentinel, asking neither
Elegy nor pity for the vast cremation
Ground that is this city.

Fanfare for All the Helping Hands

The lilies, like a brass band, march across
The living room, trumpeting their deliciousness
In brazen tones. This year the arch of
Seduction spans seas and souls, bringing
Love in pressurised litres, texts, and zoom – no
Lyrical love songs, no dulcet tones. I hear

The amaltās like a choir over a billion strong
Thundering in my heart, and in my ear
Blasts this unprecedented song, this
Unbridled declaration of the sweetness
That lies at the core. Louder than hate
And evil and maliciousness, prouder
Than the sentries guarding death's door.

What Do the Icelandic Do Without Their Pools??

When things get tricky the Icelandic aren't too picky;
They stay indoors, line up at stores,
Do their chores and mop their floors,
Report their symptoms if they start feeling peaky
Work from home and stay out of schools but
What do the Icelandic do without their pools??

Rumour has it they can't live without them
They're essential for the locals to be able to
Keep their wits about them. Babies and mothers,
Athletes, newly wed brides, and nuns, among others,
Philosophers, doctors, farmers, and fools
What do the Icelandic do without their pools?!

No soaking in the hot tubs, no water-jet back rubs,
No gossip with swimsuited friend, no kids splashing

In the shallow end, no lobster-hued legs as you go
From the forty degree hot pot to sit in the snow
No cloud of steam on shoulders bare, no dipping
Underwater to melt the icicles in your hair. No
Resolving your traumas by having a good soak,
Pandemics are one thing, but is this a joke?!

Do they raise their arms to the skies and stare
Wildly about, smother a scream and stifle a shout?
Do they refuse to eat, put down their tools? I feel
Their stress, their anguish and tension, and thus
I seek an answer to this most pertinent question:
How do they stay viking strong and keep their cools?
What do the Icelandic do without their pools?!

In Which Tyra Teaches Joey How to Be a Watchdog

So our cat is being raised by the dog.
He's learnt to tilt his head like she does
The better to hear, and she goes nervously
To him if there is any fear that someone
Is going to catch it for pushing ornaments off
The table again. No surprise then
That today he was initiated into the
Rite of Passage – or the rite of the
Lane, at any rate – the first associated

With attaining Watchdoghood: the
Guardian and Protector of the
Neighbourhood. She demonstrates the
Position on the Perch, paws out, tail
Behind. From here you can see them
She explains, go down the lane to the
Garage and into the street. In case
They need you to find them. You never know
She warns, if they'll come back. It's vital
Therefore, that we keep track.
Joey cranes his neck, tries not to make
It too apparent. He's sure he'll grow into it
But right now there's an inherent impediment:
He can't see over the balcony wall. He
Can't let on that he's not tall. Studiously
He inspects the rail. A cat can never be seen
To fail.

forging courage

Make of yourself a new city

Light I

For Keki Daruwala

It is late afternoon in early June
The sun comes into a west-facing
Room. It is summer but the sun is
Not over bright, pacing itself through
It's lengthening journey into the
Disappearing night. Grasping and
Greedy I set traps for the light.
The green of the glass to catch its
Lust; tarnished steel to hold its
Stainless dust. Found surfaces in
Kitchen space to filter and refract
It's living grace. And when I had
Exhausted all my cunning and guile
I saw that instead of entrapment
I had effected an escape. Loosed
From memory embedded in my fingers
I see before me how the late monsoon
Sun lingers after the rain somewhere
Far away the faint smell of rain on soil
Sifts through the paint and linseed oil.

Make of Yourself a New City

Paved with strangeness. Let rain
Shine your cobblestones into

Unrecognisable shapes.
If light spills from your windows leave
Your doorways shut. Unopened. Drapes
In unfamiliar textures might weave
And fold the moody skies arranged story
Upon story. Be the unwalked street
Sloshed in late-night colours. Meet
The stranger you want to be. Lie. Say
You are Courage. Named after a friend
Who has walked behind coffins. Famed
For your prowess with a gun. Claim
For yourself every outrageous falsehood
That ever fuelled a fevered fantasy. Each one
Unbelievable. Each unachievable.
How heroically you have opposed how
Selflessly you have lain yourself down
These are metal plates in my jaw I am
Too passionate that's my biggest
Flaw. Say
You are courage. You have made of yourself
A new place. An unvisited lane. Washed
In forgiveness. Given a new name.

Wild Winds

Winter leaves and Spring will too. I suppose
That's what Shelley's lines concealed

Between them, like a secret seed biding
Its time, listening with fledgling ears
To the leaflessness of snow-dry trees.
Spring will come and Summer with it and
Frozen in each year are hiding
Anniversaries of loss that bound us and
Brought us to our knees.

No Filter

Give me a world of light-shattered glass
Unreflective. No image of mountain in still
Waters. Sun-studded rivers too rippled to
Care. Water-smooth pebbles wading into
Snow, abandoning sand banks to bare not-soil,
Not-seeded, nothing yet to grow. Trees
Not needing to leaf, their thin, dark,
Selves rooted, out-flung. Give me a world
Of no coverings of colour, self-mattering,
Self-sung.

Frozen on the Way to the Sea

Arrested in free fall what visions are granted
Hurtling down the cliff face, arms flung wide
Hair streaming behind you, a flag

Of freedom, whipping away your skin no
More left to hide. How arduous the trail
From highland spring through crevice and
Gorge every opportunity to fail every
Winter-blocked path to forge. I am become
Snow I am melted from ice I am driven
Below I surface I suffice I am all in all
I have shed every motive I have ground
Every vice against the boulders I skirted
I am the fine spray of every evil ever
Found now see me fly. Shattered into
Freeze I am thrown high I am brought
To my knees I am unchosen unbeholden
I need no vision to plumb the waiting seas.

Where the Mind Is

In this house
Better than all the world, with its
Proud names and mountain cleaving
Rivers, doors shut of themselves
As we reach for wide windowed rooms.
Shutters flap and clatter in the winds
Of our hidden rage. Unsilent corners
Breathe old songs and beds creak
In our uneasy dreams. Page
After page rustles and turns, restless

In speech while ghosts the colour
Of dust sift and sigh. On sheeted
Sofas therapists resign us
To exorcists. Ah love.
How shall we arise, how go now,
When to be true to one another
Would bind us to narrow domestic
Walls where nothing shall be
Forgotten all, all, remembered.
So full of remembrances. Who once
Called us hollow? This evening spread out
Against our hurt is only an evening
After all. We are a haunted people.
Sit by my side, love, so stubbornly
Leaving. Cleaving together let us sit
In the shelter of this woven shawl.

An Amaltās Poem

You can pick them off pavements
On an early morning walk, the bright
Yellow heralding the noonday avatar
Of the shy pink dawn. You can bear
Them in arms as you head home,
A Joan of Arc taking the fire into
Her own hands to burn in memory
Bowls. Remember how it bloomed

When we were locked, imprisoned,
Roomed; how it blazed like swords
Of justice, unseen, ignored, while we
Did battle with our bare hands alone,
Unmoored. Ah Amaltās. Beauty is
Truth, they say. While we glory
In your gladness, light headed with
Summer madness, what epiphany
Do you bring us that will light us
On our way?

Among Walls

They are just squares of light
After all. Painted over in shades
Of indoor selves – kitchenyellow,
Teenagelavender, adultwhite. Wall
To wall something of winter
Remains, even now, in the sprung
Blue, even here, in the woodveins,
Even auroral, gleaming, even
Unangular you, absently leaning,
Planning, already autumn in
Your head, the summer a mosaic
Of coloured squares, bright facings,
Pages of days and nights unread.
If we replaced these walls with

Others, how they stood, their
Colours, what would they then
Enclose? When the bright wash
Of sun flows in from the vast
Outdoors, what will we have asked
Of these that we won't get from
Those?

The Day the Music

To each day its song; to each year
Its notes, high and graceful, low
And strong. To each hour its departing,
Its arrival, its gifting, granting to
The next its instrument, its muse.
Ivory so steadfast beside ebony
Remains true to the pathetique as
To the jingle of childhood. Use, its
Only heart and soul. Such a braveheart
Trundling out on the road again
Another home another hand another
Spot in which to stand. It lies
Back, free, fragile as spring snow
Open as the skies; ready to be
Retuned, unafraid of goodbyes.

Skálagerði Fimm

It's that time of day. The sun
Comes in, sloping down
Hlíðarfjall, through Glerárdalur,
Shining across Glerár itself,
River mirror. Súlur salutes
It's passing, flying a sun banner
Along it's southwest flank,
Flagging it on down to slip
Through the gap where the fir
Used to stand in the far corner
Of the lawn. The light pauses
On the porch, too mellow to
Scorch the level planks, dark
Wood, breathes in deep and
Slow and exhales gently through
The curtains lacework sieve,
Sifting the years laid long along
It's golden floors, gilding bare
Surfaces where things used
To be, taking its time taking
It's leave.

Who Ate My Mountain??

Did you take a bite out of that hill? I ask
The suspicious looking duck. It eyes me
Balefully. Does that look like my bill? Chastened,
I turn to the annoyed goose, who fixes
My shins in its sights. Did you eat
My mountain, I ask, before deciding against
Interrogating its bites. I'll take that
As a no, I mutter, turning to the wide
Wings that flutter into view. The swan
Swivels its long neck about. Apparently
It's a lot to chew. I catch the wind,
The sky, the cloud, hold them
In my fist and demand aloud
That they confess and explain
The mouth-shaped absence
Of a snowy peak. They regard
The human with their air-shaped
Eyes. Have you never heard
A mountain speak?

Move Backwards Into Beauty

Move backwards into beauty. Catch yourself
By surprise. Stumble into the trance-like
Grey of a cloudy sea, the blue-streaked

Hills, the rare sunrise. What sign could
Warn of sudden breathlessness? What
Words signal the sucker punch of
Remembrances? Move backwards
But beware a beauty that steals
Up behind you and wraps its arms
Around your waist and snuggles
Its face in your neck, a snare.
What would you have the signpost
Do – caution that memory away
From you? Move backwards, one
Foot behind the other; time enough
To be forewarned once you're there.

Reckonings

White is for the Spring snow, awaiting
The common snipe's signal: to go, to
Leave, to sift through the sand as the
Wind through the snipe's feathered
Sieve. To thread its melting paleness
Into the seasons' weave. Green is
For the unmelted ice, glowing
Under the sea. A savouring of
The preserving salts, a submerged
Fantasy. To underlie, to undergo
A trans-mortality. Grey is for the

Here and now, shallow ripples across
The deep. Oceans of nonchalance, an
Indifferent indignity. How quick we are
To judge, it says, winter's inevitable
Thaw. Is death-to-life so worthy of
Praise, life-to-death such a flaw?

In Defence of Shiny Things

Though much is taken, much abides.
Sometimes that old man's solace
Is hard to find. Let loose in a world
Of losing, small tokens of gladness
Should be bulwarked against the
Typhoons, the eddies, the solar flares
Of sadness. Bricks and sandbags
Tied up with string, ribboned and
Ruched, battlements of glitter and
Bling. It is a gift, that which abides.
The shiny thing in which random
Senseless, arbitrary, beauty resides.
Put it in his hands, though he resists.
Wrap it and write a card though she
Insists she is not a child and too old
For this. Give it anyway, though it
Consists of no more than a thought.
Persist.

Silver Linings

The wind was in our faces, the sun
At our backs. On the horizon, blue-white
Traces of the mystic mountain, a
Reminding of permanence. The ocean
Rippling with silver. The path lightly
Winding. At the lighthouse, men
Are fishing, the long lines searching,
Finding silver fins flashing, bright
Laces. Our steps fall together, never
Minding the tips and turns in the road.
Every year lies beneath the other,
A lining, a strength underneath each
Other, a sheet of love, a binding.

For All the Students Who Remind Us to Stand Tall

Three syllables it's a clarion call
Azadi
From every bomb about to fall
Azadi
Between the bricks of every wall
Azadi
Mass grave and shrouded head
Broken spire and emptied bed

What if every pebble in piled up
Rubble every open grit-filled crack
Lipped blood toothed mouth said
Azadi?
What was it the sirens sang
That stouthearted heroes tied
Their hands and ordered deafness
On the unthinking bands of labouring
Common stock sailors? Were they singing
Azadi
Did he see them bringing
Azadi
Watch them wrenching, wringing
Azadi
From the clenched fists of jailers?
Who will heed this
Azadi
Help to speed this
Azadi
Make their creed, this
Azadi
Ring out tyranny and
Ring in
Azadi!

What Glory

of stained glass,
Glow of candles, fan vaulted heavens,
Dreams of spires, singing bell towers,
What wings of buttresses flying can
Compare with this, a cathedral
Of our joy.
You can sing your hymns of gladness
You can pace your temple rounds
You can sway in divine ecstasies
And swoon to religious grounds.
But give me a moment of hysterics
Giggling arm in arm. Helpless
From happy giddiness, unsteady
From juvenile silliness, a picture
Of family found.

Mater Dolorosa

Who decides the colours of grief.
When were the shades of mourning
Decreed. The Hindu whites the
Christian blacks, whose customs of
Adorning the body of sorrow
Are we doomed conditioned fore-given

To follow? What mother's face
Shrouded against mercy turned away
From grace impossible to behold
Desperate to enfold wraps itself
In the deep blue of impossible loss
And the soundless boundless suffering
Of gold.

Fire in the Sky

There are no portents, the Earth
Is clear on that. If stone melting
Fire is too much for you, pretend
It's an anger that sears your heart.
If continents moving miles beneath
This too solid ground are felt in
The gripping soles of your feet
Think of it as lovers being pulled
Apart. But when you hear the heat
Singeing the colours of the night,
Think. The Earth doesn't deal
In symbols, omens, literary things.
She breaks, she cracks, she makes
New lands. You are shaken, you fall,
You kneel, yield; you and pirates and
Children and kings. Consider the taken,

The broken, the rubble-buried hands.
Consider the songs in the ashes of
Your fields.

The Poet Wishes to Write of Joy

Joy is a haiku
Its timing is exquisite
Birdsong in the night.
A heaping of blades of gold shining
Like a haystack. A heartbreak of falcons in
Flight. Joy is a reaching, a metaphor
A thread in the needle of desire.
Risking blood in the need to
Hold, daring your heart to lie
On the pyre, a piercing to the core.
May falcons fill and fire your sight
Your heart a beacon to the burning.
May songbirds sing your harvests to light
And hay fields blaze your yearning.

Laccolith*

Show me a mountain and I
Will show you the liquid red fingers
That pushed the land apart. Show me a peak

Mighty against the sky and I
Will show you the weak, time-weathered
Rock that fell away, exposing its heart. Your
Unbelieving eye might admire the glow of
Snow freshly fallen. Allow me to show you
The freshly fallen. Thirty three thousand,
One hundred and one, as of today.
Six million from '96, fifteen thousand till Christmas
Last. Hands in unspoken of lands. Once black
Or brown or skintones unknown, all red
Now. Show me a mountain, an extrusion of
Bone. Call it a testament to Time.
I will show you how the history of the Earth
Will be written by your hands and mine.

**Laccoliths are formed by rising magma that force strata apart, raising it to form peaks or domes that remain standing long after the softer rock around them has fallen away.*

City of the Torch Bearer

I heard Lady Liberty
Caught lightning last night.
I heard she was tired of bearing
A light nobody saw. That arm
Must ache from the pain of
Nobody looking up, nobody

Coming in, under her sheltering
Frame. Not the hungry not
The maimed. No tired and bruised
War-torn and refused. You see
Her here against a sky of blue.
Her familiar silhouette
Coloured with rue. She must
Regret being unfairly used.
I heard the earth shook
Under her feet yesterday.
She mad. If I lived in her town I'd
Get the hell out've her way.

Light II

It could be glass it could be metal
I guess some things seem more
Special in the light. A cooling
Blue a flash of gold a sudden
Something the heart could hold
Long after it's vanished from
Sight. A clock a vase a flower
Memento mori assert the passing
Of each luminous hour when in fact
The limited lives of things is
Never in doubt. The slow burn
Singeing the edges of joy lend

Beauty to its truth and yet
What need of words or Grecian
Urn when we are bent on the slaughter
Of languages, books, temples,
Homes, refuges, children, youth
And age. The ugliness of truth
Lies everywhere. It could be glass
It could be metal. What light what
Flash of gold what page handwritten
Hand painted will ignite
Its beauty and give us its ashes
To hold.

Bird's-eye Beach

Hunger is an eagle in a sunburst silhouette;
Waves on the shore, rippling riddles
Decoded into fish, silver ciphers of some
Larger mystery the hunter has no
Interest in. The ocean, ever compassionate,
Deciphers every wish, an offering each
Creature may invest in. Crows hop
Its shores convivially sharing
The community feast of little finned-ones,
Each wee, timorous beast granted such
Pitying immunity that its sky-seeing eye
Is blind to the ignominious peck of life's

Slings and arrows. Still in the shallows
We, pressing our feet into the forgiving
Sand the waters wash clean. No cleaner
For all the hunger and hunting we
Have seen.

Because I Shall Never Stand Here Again

When does the leaving start? Not
With that last hug, the receding
Figures waving, watching you
Depart. Not when you stand with
Your bags as the automatic doors
Slide silently apart, nor even as you
Step into your new life your new
House your new job your new
Friends holding out their hands
To take you into their fold. No.
For all these you forge a new
Heart. This is not even close
To the start. All this you can hold.
Leaving begins when you return.
To the walls the faces the always-known
Smells of sheets and dishes and
Stairwells and mealtime voices
And night time rituals and
Comfortable places. All those

Impossibly arched bridges
That you never thought to burn.
You have never really left
Till going back snatches
That old heart out of your
Migratory body leaving you
Truly bereft.

'There is a crack, a crack in everything'

See how neatly they fit together, the
Pieces of the sky. Like the lids of Rubbermaid
Boxes. And indeed, here we are, you and
I, enclosed with our things, carefully
Collected and placed so that even if
There's some accidental shaking, there's
No chance of anything breaking. Our things
Will cushion us, we will protect each other
From our sharp edges but isn't it strange
The way those triangles like cosmic
Wedges rise and dive to come together
And shut. I wonder why they lifted
Them open, those that put us in.
Just checking, maybe, that nothing's
Shifted. No, we're ok, everything's
Here – our faces, our hands, our
Goodness, our wars, our utterly

Unoriginal sin. I'm glad some of the
Light fell through the cracks, though,
And lightened the air in our packed down
Bin.

'That's how the light gets in'

The moon's a deft cleaver. She uses
A variety of knives. Some serrated –
As you see demonstrated in
The uneven edges of the clouds
Separated – some smaller, more
Scalpel-like. Sometimes its more
Her own head on a long, thin, spike
(I'm resisting, mightily, the seductive
Sign with a temptingly placed
Bike!). But to be fair, the poet is
Not all about the exploited metaphor.
It's just her job to wield her knife
Deftly, find a way to break
The skin. That's how the light
Gets in.

'Who Wants to Live Forever'

There's never a straight answer.
The spirit yearns to follow futures
Of the heart. To hover over cradles,
To sift through their fingers grasping
Honours, to light their eyes, be part
Of bearing griefs. But the body lingers,
Doesn't it, reluctant to let be
To let go to let alone, denying itself
Relief. There's never
A straight path to that question,
Is there: who wants to live
Forever. How to get through today
How face tomorrow but you know
Things will get better. You know this
Because you see it get worse. And
Because Freddie, mercurially gifted,
Sings, still, in your head, and Beauty,
Like Hope, doesn't deal in nows and
Sooner or laters. It lives in
Forevers instead.

Leiðhamrar, The Cliff on The Way

It's the house at the end of the lane
But the lane is not the end. It opens

Onto the cliff edge – hamrar, there
Is no good translation of the word -
More a bend, a rounded rocky
Wedge like a knuckly hand resting
On a knee, bristle and vein
Sloping to the fingertip. Our house
Sits somewhere on the wrist.
And so I said to the husband – leave
The lights on a little longer. It's
Past the new year – alright, it's
March. He gives me the arch look
By which to convey that the neighbours
Had long since switched off and put
Theirs away. It's not the end
Of the lane, I say. Think of it as being
The glow that lights the walker's
Way as they trudge out of the ocean
(We're on a cliff) out of snow that
Might lie hidden, might lie low. Up
From the tracks that rise precipitously
Our's will be the first light they'll see.
I can't say he appreciated the poetic
License. But he let the fairy lights glimmer
On the fence.

Ice Circles in the Harbour

Maybe its low tide and you're feeling
Less submerged. Water rising doesn't
Manage the same confidence as might
The sun, burning star though it be.
I've seen ducks swimming in long lines
Navigating between ice patches on
The sea. As if the crinkle-edged circles
Emerged from the shallows only to
Show you how easily the ocean floats
On its own uneasy surface. No wave
No crest no pillowing billows cradling
To rest your uneasy soul that nature
Doesn't care to save. Ducks get through
It. So could you. Maybe paddling is
All it takes to be brave.

Courage IX

When we find shells we'll put them
In something braided, maybe wicker.
Pine cones – the tender baby ones –
Might be snug in that old bread basket
The one with the faded linen, maybe
Something thicker. I've been thinking
About those bright coasters we saved

From your mothers house, how they've
Staved off the knowing that she's gone.
How mine would've repotted her plants
Knowing I can't keep anything green
Alive. In the hive of my mind I've
Slotted each keeping each holding each
Thing within another, wrapped, entrapped,
Kept against the day when courage
Will prise, surprise, my fingers open and
Say look. Open your eyes. It's not going
Away.

Volcanoes in the Spring

Now moves the earth beneath our feet. Now
Speaks the stone in tongues of heat. How
Still the sea that tempests bears yet
Folds to its heart the hulls of fleets.
Now sheds the birch its crimson bark. Now
Treads the half light into dark. How
Comes it home, this ceaseless street, that
Traffics in hope, that finds its mark.
Now ask me not for chariots of fire.
I cannot make the peace you desire.
I fashion boats of paper – embark
And float your joy on words and mire.

Made in Heaven

Will you marry me, said
The heavens to the earth. You're
Solid and I'm not. There isn't
Anything you want that
I've got. But we'd make
A decent pair – your
Earth, water, and fire
To my air.
The mountains, already asleep,
Didn't respond. Maybe
They couldn't be bothered
By a proposal so errantly
Superficial. The rivers shivered.
They moved too swiftly
To consider making any
Mating official. The volcanoes,
Just done erupting, busy
Soothing fire to rock thought
The heavens rude for
Interrupting and rolled
A fiery eye.
The extended hand remains.
Perhaps some stargazing,
Moondreaming, sunstunned
Passerby will look up when
The heavens burst and it rains.

Vatnshlíðarvatn

A lake named after itself

Sapphire hard, diamond edged,
The rivers cut through
The snow burnt grasses, pale beige
Soft faun. The car speeds, too,
The bright day too suddenly summer
No time to green, just swathes
Of blue. Once when I was tiny
I fell into a lake amidst picnic
Foods and rugs and chatter. I have
No memory of this – maybe
It was my sister. We pass an impossible
Lake, a curved jewel set in
Matching mountains blue and white.
Stop, stop, I say, I never get a
Good picture of this, we have time
Today. When I was little I was nearly
Swept out to sea, bent over a shell
As the wave curved over and
Cradled me into its lap. I can feel
The clutched sand rush away
From my fingers though I have
No memory of being saved.
Yet here I am. Gathering bits of
Myself together. Assembling

Them to look like a work of art.
When I was much older
He gave me a wispy feather.
I don't know what you could
Do with it, he said. But I know
Your heart.

When You Run Out of Words

Say this to the heartbroken
People: all shall not be well
Till you are well. When speech
Is stolen from your mouth
And no sound comes from
Your throat, say this
To the embattled people, the
Battered and shackled
People: all shall not be well
Till you are well. Poets
Have said that you should speak
Because your lips, your tongue
Are free and the truth lives still.
Then say this to those watching
Over their dead, to the martyred
The sainted the disintegrated
Healers in hell. Say it wherever
And whenever your voice

Has no choice but to say
What needs to be said: all
Shall not be well
Till you are well.

Acknowledgements

To Abhivyakti Singh, for first visualising this collection: you are the editor all poets should have. And the Hachette team who works miracles. Thank you. To Thomas Abraham, as always, for laughing at me and believing in me: I am indebted in equal measure for both.

To Kári Stefánsson, for being my literary sounding board and friend, for lunchtime advice and suggestions that shaped this book: thank you. To Paul Kane, for the grace of his time, insight, and advice: I am truly grateful.

To Anannya Dasgupta: fifteen years ago, you gave me the courage to start writing, and every year since, the space and community to continue through everything the years brought. You have created and nurtured a community of poets who write together, suffer and rejoice together, and read and recite together. My gratitude to you runs deep.

And so to the Daily Riyaaz community: brought together by Anannya but coming together each year, you have shifted my idea of the creative process itself. Far from the ivory tower of the lonely head of the poet, you have taught me that poetry happens in community. April comes as a benediction and release for me, a time and space in which to unpack the terror and euphoria of the universe surrounded by kindness and empathy. Everyone should have you. Thank you.

And thus, my gratitude to the communities that have made this collection possible: to Randi Stebbins, who first insisted I think of myself as a writer, and to the Ós Pressan community she created who first brought me into the fold of Icelandic poets. To Ewa Marcinek and Natasha Stolyarova, who invited me into the community of foreign writers in Iceland, a community that shared their foreignness and made our writing a home. To Stephen Lárus and the Myndlistaskóli community of artists who gave me a whole new poetic vocabulary through painting. To the community of friends and extended family on Facebook who were my first audience when I felt brave enough to write and whose encouragement has meant the world to me. To the Coven, who will know what I mean when I say that their community feels like magic.

My longstanding and undying appreciation for Gunnar Pálsson, who has taken it upon himself to be proud of my poetry on behalf of his parents and mine, and without whom nothing I publish ever gets to the properly formatted stage. To my daughters, Arshia Eyrún and Ashali Ásrún, you are all the courage and beauty I will ever need. And as ever, my gratitude to my family who, despite demanding decoding keys to my poems, has been proud of anything I wrote from the time I was six.

Paintings Courtesy

1. Front cover painting: 'Sunlight in the South Room at Kellie Castle,' 1913, by John Henry Lorimer (1856–1936). Oil on canvas. 102 × 64 cm (40.1 × 25.1 in). Source: Wikimedia Commons.
2. Back cover painting: 'A Sunlit Interior with Summer Flowers on a Ledge', between 1885 and 1945, by Wilhelm Andersen (1867–1945). Oil on canvas. 62.2 x 72.2 cm (24.4 x 28.4 in). Source: Wikimedia Commons.
3. 'The Prospect of Loss': 'A Sunlit Interior,' between 1889-1942, by Hans Hilsøe (1871–1942). Oil on canvas. 51 x 40 cm (20 x 15.7 in). Source: Wikimedia Commons.
4. 'Loosing and Binding': 'Sunlit Interior,' 1934, by Robert Panitzsch (1879–1949). Oil on canvas. 60 x 49 cm (23.6 x 19.2 in). Source: Wikimedia Commons.
5. 'Lost and Bound': 'Sunshine in the room. Springtime.' 1935, by Robert Panitzsch (1879–1949). Oil on canvas. 60 x 50 cm (23.6 x 19.6 in). Source: Wikimedia Commons.
6. 'If The Brave Were Legion': 'Frozen Lake,' 2018, Giti Chandra. Oil on canvas. 24 x 30 cm. Source: author's archive.
7. 'Forging Courage': 'Café Terrace at Night,' 16 September 1888, by Vincent van Gogh (1853–1890). Oil on canvas. 81 x 65.5 cm (31.8 x 25.7 in). Source: Wikimedia Commons.

MORE FROM

HACHETTE INDIA POETRY SERIES

Rooted in landscapes and listening, Siddhartha Menon's *Lone Pine* is a vivid meditation on topography, time and the shifting nature of identity. The poems move with grace and intensity, carrying the reader from stillness to revelation, from the immediate to the far-flung.

In 'Settings', the quiet residence of trees and ceaseless motion of the river offer more than scenery – they embody questions of belonging, conflict and nature's flawed and unyielding beauty. With 'Stirrings', the focus turns inward, tracing the currents of human connection, the ebb and flow of relationships, and the pulse of time moving through us. 'Bearings' asks what it means to see and to turn away, to bear witness to violence, personal and planetary, or to find meaning in silence. In these poems, Menon stands at the threshold: observer, participant, seeker of truth.

With language both tender and unflinching, *Lone Pine* offers no easy answers, but an invitation to watch and listen. It nudges us to navigate the world – its rough contours, its shadows and its light – and to discover the shape of our own place within it.

RAISING READERS
Books Build Bright Futures

Dear Reader,

We hope you enjoyed reading this book and we'd love your attention for one more page, to share with you what's going on with children and books.

The number of children reading in their leisure time and for fun is in rapid decline. Young people have a lot of competition for their time, and a worryingly high number have only a few or no books at home.

If this is not a crisis already, it soon will be.

Studies have shown that reading for fun is the **single biggest predictor of a child's future success** – more than family circumstance, parents' educational background or income. It improves academic results, mental health, wealth, communication skills and ambition.

Our business works committedly to create books that are well-researched, engaging, and enduring, but here are some ways we can all raise more readers:

- Reading to children for just 10 minutes a day makes a difference
- Don't give up if children aren't regular readers – it's not just about the number of books they have or read but about encouraging interest and engagement
- Encourage them to listen to audiobooks
- Support schools and other libraries
- Give books as gifts

Thank you for reading: there's a lot more information about how to encourage children to read on our website.

www.raisingreaders.in